The Life of Christ in Poetry

The Life of Christ

IN POETRY

COMPILED BY HAZEL DAVIS CLARK

A selection from CHRIST IN POETRY *which was compiled and edited by Thomas Curtis Clark and Hazel Davis Clark*

ASSOCIATION PRESS · NEW YORK

THE LIFE OF CHRIST IN POETRY

———

Copyright © 1957 by
National Board of Young Men's Christian Associations

———

Association Press, 291 Broadway, New York 7, N. Y.

Price, 50 cents

Library of Congress catalog card number: 57-5495

 475

Printed in the United States of America

Contents

5

THE MAN CHRIST JESUS

THE WAY OF THE CROSS

THE CONTINUING CALVARY

RESURRECTION

COME, FOLLOW ME

THE CONTINUING CHRIST

THE REVOLUTIONIST

THE LOST CHRIST

THE TRIUMPHANT CHRIST

PREFACE

BROUGHT UP in the home of a minister, I early learned the story of Christ. The Christ my father preached was no mystical being, far from our weak humanity. He was the Christ so vividly portrayed in the Gospels, the close Friend, the ministering Servant; One who spent his later years talking with people who had problems—the lame and halt, lonely, bewildered men and women; One who found joy in taking little children into his arms. My minister-father was not a product of any school of theology. He had been a carpenter, and his later education was derived from a "secular" university. But he did preach about "the Man Christ Jesus."

It is largely this friendly, sympathetic Christ, "the lover of women and men"—the Christ my father preached—who is portrayed in this book. The poets of recent decades have seen Christ in the same way; and the poets are excellent interpreters of Christ, who also was a poet.

As poetry editor for the *Christian Century* for more than a quarter-century, I had the privilege of passing editorially on much of the better religious poetry that has been written during the exciting years since the First World War. We have included in this anthology the best of these *Christian Century* poems that portray "the Christ who enters our door," the Christ who said, "I am among you as one that serveth" and "I have called you friends."

To the tributes of prophets and apostles, of philos-

11

ophers and sages, has now been added the testimony of the poets; and the more recent singers claim a place in this great congregation of worshipers. They have told of the Man Christ Jesus, for they feel that his glorious humanity may have been overlooked. Having seen the friendly, human Christ through their rapt eyes, we shall certainly go forward to a still higher view: we shall see him as our Divine Lord and Saviour. How else can his human superiority be explained?

THOMAS CURTIS CLARK

[Thomas Curtis Clark is not with us now. His widow, Mrs. Hazel Clark, has helped to select from *Christ in Poetry* these poems for the shorter Reflection Book.]

ACKNOWLEDGMENTS

ACKNOWLEDGMENT is hereby gratefully made of the generous co-operation of both contributing poets and publishers in the compilation of this anthology. The compilers have made every effort to trace the ownership of all copyrighted poems. To the best of their knowledge they have secured all necessary permissions from authors or their authorized agents, or from both. Should there be a question regarding the use of any poem, regret is expressed for unconscious error.

So far as possible the styling—punctuation, spelling, capitalization, and so forth—conforms to that found in original standard versions. This explains the variations in the text of the anthology.

Permission has been received, either from the poets or from their estates, for the inclusion of poems by the following authors: Katharine Lee Bates, Dwight Bradley, William E. Brooks, Ralph Cheyney, Leslie Savage Clark, Stanton A. Coblentz, Ernest Cadman Colwell, Franklin D. Elmer, Jr., Harold E. Fey, Natalie Flohr, Florence Kiper Frank, Herbert D. Gallaudet, Winfred Ernest Garrison, Molly Anderson Haley, Mary Hallett, Georgia Harkness, Una W. Harsen, Sara Henderson Hay, William H. Hudnut, Jr., Lilith Lorraine, Edwin Markham, John Oxenham, Edith Lovejoy Pierce, Edwin McNeill Poteat, E. Merrill Root, Rolland W. Schloerb, William J. Suckow, Ruby Weyburn Tobias, Lucia Trent, Carl S. Weist, Robert Whitaker.

13

Sincere thanks are due the following publishers for granting permission to use poems by the authors indicated:

Harper and Brothers: poems by G. A. Studdert-Kennedy.

Houghton Mifflin Company: poems by Longfellow and Lowell from their *Complete Poetical Works*.

Bruce Humphries, Inc.: poems by Ida Norton Munson.

The Macmillan Company: poems by Robert Browning and Alfred Tennyson from their *Collected Works*.

Charles Scribner's Sons: excerpt from "The Toiling of Felix," reprinted from *The Poems of Henry van Dyke;* copyright 1911 by Charles Scribner's Sons, 1939 by Tertius van Dyke; used by permission of the publishers.

The *Christian Century,* in which publication many of the poems included first appeared.

THE COMPILERS

Nativity

BEFORE THE PALING OF THE STARS

Before the paling of the stars,
  Before the winter morn,
Before the earliest cockcrow,
  Jesus Christ was born:
Born in a stable,
  Cradled in a manger,
In the world his hands had made
  Born a stranger.

Priest and king lay fast asleep
  In Jerusalem,
Young and old lay fast asleep
  In crowded Bethlehem;
Saint and Angel, ox and ass,
  Kept a watch together
Before the Christmas daybreak
  In the winter weather.

Jesus on his mother's breast
  In the stable cold,
Spotless Lamb of God was he,
  Shepherd of the fold:
Let us kneel with Mary maid,
  With Joseph bent and hoary,
With Saint and Angel, ox and ass,
  To hail the King of Glory.

CHRISTINA G. ROSSETTI

FROM "HAMLET"

Some say that ever 'gainst that season comes
Wherein our Saviour's birth is celebrated,
The bird of dawning singeth all night long:
And then, they say, no spirit can walk abroad;
The nights are wholesome; then no planets strike,
No fairy takes, nor witch hath power to charm;
So hallow'd and so gracious is the time.

WILLIAM SHAKESPEARE

THE KINGS OF THE EAST

The Kings of the East are riding
  Tonight to Bethlehem.
The sunset glows dividing,
The Kings of the East are riding;
A star their journey guiding,
  Gleaming with gold and gem
The Kings of the East are riding
  Tonight to Bethlehem.

.   .   .   .   .

There beams above a manger
  The child-face of a star;
Amid the stars a stranger,
It beams above a manger;
What means this ether-ranger
  To pause where poor folk are?
There beams above a manger
  The child-face of a star.

KATHARINE LEE BATES

THREE GIFTS

Gold and frankincense and myrrh,
    Lord, they brought to Thee;
And myrrh was death, and incense prayer,
    And gold was victory.
But first is last as last was first;
The myrrh they gave Thee in Thy thirst
    Upon the tree.
And through the solemn centuries
    The prayers of saints have risen
From hearth and chancel, crypt and tomb,
    From pyre and from prison.
Now never was the mystic power
    Of the gold fulfilled;
Yet draweth on the mighty hour
    By the Father willed
When every knee shall bow to him
    Who on the cross was lift,
And every tongue acclaim him king;
    This is the golden gift.

                 EDWARD JUDSON HANNA

THREE WISE KINGS

To Bethlehem town in the long ago
Three Kings of the East came riding;
Over the plains where the hot sands glow,
And over the mountains deep in snow,
Seeking the King in the manger low—
Three Kings of the East a-riding.

To the inn they came, to the common room,
And they bowed them low before him;
And spices and gold and rare perfume
They piled at his feet in the gathering gloom,
But the Christ-Child's eyes lit up the room,
As he smiled at the gray heads o'er him.

Then into the night to their lands afar,
The bells on their camels ringing,
They took their way where the wide plains are;
But gone from the sky was the Christmas star,
And strangely gone were the fears that mar,
While peace in their hearts was singing.

And ever as dawns the Christmas Day,
The worn old world goes faring,
Seeking the place where the young Child lay,
Where the Kings of the East bowed low to pray,
And peace was born to abide alway,
In hearts that were long despairing.

WILLIAM E. BROOKS

A CHRISTMAS CAROL

"What means this glory 'round our feet,"
    The Magi mused, "more bright than morn?"
And voices chanted clear and sweet,
    "Today the Prince of Peace is born!"

"What means that star," the shepherds said,
    "That brightens through the rocky glen?"
And angels, answering overhead,
    Sang, "Peace on earth, good-will to men!"

'Tis eighteen hundred years and more
    Since those sweet oracles were dumb;
We wait for him, like them of yore;
    Alas, he seems so slow to come.

But it was said in words of gold,
    No time or sorrow e'er shall dim,
That little children might be bold
    In perfect trust to come to Him.

All 'round about our feet shall shine
    A light like that the wise men saw,
If we our willing hearts incline
    To that sweet Life which is the Law.

So shall we learn to understand
    The simple faith of shepherds then,
And, kindly clasping hand in hand,
    Sing, "Peace on earth, good-will to men."

For they who to their childhood cling,
    But keep their natures fresh as morn,
Once more shall hear the angels sing,
    "Today the Prince of Peace is born!"

                            JAMES RUSSELL LOWELL

NO ROOM

Once when they gathered long ago
    At taxing time, in David's town,
The village inn was crowded so
    With those who laid large monies down,
There was no room except a stall
    Back yonder where the cattle were,
When Mary came, the blest of all—
    No room, though God had chosen her.

And what if in these taxing times,
    Our land, the whole world's inn of old,
Is crowded so with men whose crimes
    Have filled their pilfering palms with gold,
And with their slavish retinues
    Of serving maids and serving men—
What if, when God bends low to choose,
    His choice shall find no room again?

                                    ROBERT WHITAKER

INCARNATE LOVE

Love came down at Christmas,
    Love all lovely, Love Divine;
Love was born at Christmas,
    Star and Angels gave the sign.

Worship we the Godhead,
    Love incarnate, Love Divine;
Worship we our Jesus:
    But wherewith for sacred sign?

Love shall be our token,
  Love be yours and Love be mine,
Love to God and all men,
  Love for plea and gift and sign.
CHRISTINA G. ROSSETTI

THERE'S A SONG IN THE AIR!

There's a song in the air!
  There's a star in the sky!
There's a mother's deep prayer
  And a baby's low cry!
And the star rains its fire while the beautiful sing,
For the manger of Bethlehem cradles a King!

There's a tumult of joy
  O'er the wonderful birth,
For the Virgin's sweet boy
  Is the Lord of the earth.
Ay! the star rains its fire while the beautiful sing,
For the manger of Bethlehem cradles a King!

In the light of the star
  Lie the ages impearled;
And that song from afar
  Has swept over the world
Every hearth is aflame, and the beautiful sing
In the homes of the nations that Jesus is King.

We rejoice in the light,
   And we echo the song
That comes down through the night
   From the heavenly throng.
Ay! we shout to the lovely evangel they bring,
And we greet in his cradle our Saviour and King!
JOSIAH GILBERT HOLLAND

CHRISTMAS

As shadows cast by cloud and sun
   Flit o'er the summer grass,
So, in thy sight, Almighty One,
   Earth's generations pass.
And as the years, an endless host,
   Come swiftly pressing on,
The brightest names that earth can boast
   Just glisten and are gone.

Yet doth the star of Bethlehem shed
   A luster pure and sweet:
And still it leads, as once it led,
   To the Messiah's feet.
O Father, may that holy star
   Grow every year more bright,
And send its glorious beams afar
   To fill the world with light.
WILLIAM CULLEN BRYANT

DECEMBER TWENTY-FOURTH

Tomorrow you are born again
    Who died so many times.
Do you like the candle-light,
    Do you like the chimes?

Do you stop to wonder
    Why men never see
How very closely Bethlehem
    Approaches Calvary?
                ELEANOR SLATER

IN THINE OWN HEART

Though Christ a thousand **times**
    In Bethlehem be born,
If he's not born in thee
    Thy soul is still forlorn.
The cross on Golgotha
    Will never save thy soul,
The cross in thine own heart
    Alone can make thee whole.
                ANGELUS SILESIUS

THE SHEPHERD SPEAKS

Out of the midnight sky a great dawn broke,
And a voice singing flooded us with song.
In David's city was He born, it sang,
A Saviour, Christ the Lord. Then while I sat
Shivering with the thrill of that great cry,
A mighty choir a thousandfold more sweet
Suddenly sang, Glory to God, and Peace—
Peace on the earth; my heart, almost unnerved
By that swift loveliness, would hardly beat.
Speechless we waited till the accustomed night
Gave us no promise more of sweet surprise;
Then scrambling to our feet, without a word
We started through the fields to find the Child.

JOHN ERSKINE

In Nazareth

THE LITTLE CHILD

A simple-hearted Child was He,
   And He was nothing more;
In summer days, like you and me,
   He played about the door,
Or gathered, when the father toiled,
   The shavings from the floor.

Sometimes He lay upon the grass,
   The same as you and I,
And saw the hawks above Him pass
   Like specks against the sky;
Or, clinging to the gate, He watched
   The stranger passing by.

A simple Child, and yet, I think,
   The bird-folk must have known,
The sparrow and the bobolink,
   And claimed Him for their own,
And gathered round Him fearlessly
   When He was all alone.

The lark, the linnet, and the dove,
   The chaffinch and the wren,
They must have known His watchful love
   And given their worship then;
They must have known and glorified
   The Child who died for men.

And when the sun at break of day
   Crept in upon His hair,
I think it must have left a ray
   Of unseen glory there—
A kiss of love on that little brow
   For the thorns that it must wear.

ALBERT BIGELOW PAINE

THE CARPENTER

Silent at Joseph's side he stood,
And smoothed and trimmed the shapeless wood.
And with firm hand, assured and slow,
Drove in each nail with measured blow.

Absorbed, he planned a wooden cask,
Nor asked for any greater task;
Content to make, with humble tools,
Tables and little children's stools.

Lord, give me careful hands to make
Such simple things as for Thy sake.
Happy within Thine House to dwell
If I may make one table well.

PHYLLIS HARTNOLL

THE CARPENTER

I wonder what he charged for chairs at Nazareth
And did men try to beat him down
And boast about it in the town—
"I bought it cheap for half-a-crown
From that mad Carpenter"?

And did they promise and not pay,
Put it off to another day;
O, did they break his heart that way,
My Lord, the Carpenter?

I wonder did he have bad debts,
And did he know my fears and frets?
The gospel writer here forgets
To tell about the Carpenter.

But that's just what I want to know.
Ah! Christ in glory, here below
Men cheat and lie to one another so;
It's hard to be a carpenter.

G. A. STUDDERT-KENNEDY

YOUNG MAN IN A GALILEAN DOORWAY

Yes, utterly he loves his Nazareth:
The dusty village sprawling in the sun;
Rows of white houses harboring one by one
The hearts of plodding folk whom life and death
Receive as simply as their daily breath;
The dancing feet of children as they run
To meet him and entreat him share their fun;
Child eyes as wide as blue Gennesareth,
Deeper with wonder; fields of ripening grain;
New lilies; ox yokes smoothed of gall and pain;
The cool, clean workshop redolent of wood
And toil; the hill where dawn's first visions brood,
Beckoning to prayer like flags of hope unfurled:
He loves all that. And God so loves the world.

HERBERT D. GALLAUDET

IN THE CARPENTER SHOP

I wish I had been his apprentice,
   To see him each morning at seven,
As he tossed his gray tunic about him,
   The Master of earth and of heaven;
When he lifted the lid of his work chest
   And opened his carpenter's kit,
And looked at his chisels and augers,
   And took the bright tools out of it;
When he gazed at the rising sun tinting
   The dew on the opening flowers,
And he smiled at the thought of his Father
   Whose love floods this fair world of ours;
When he fastened the apron about him,
   And put on his workingman's cap,
And grasped the smooth haft of his hammer
   To give the bent woodwork a tap,
Saying, "Lad, let us finish this ox yoke,
   The farmer must finish his crop."
Oh, I wish I had been his apprentice
   And worked in the Nazareth shop.

ANONYMOUS

CARPENTER OF ETERNITY

A carpenter, he worked with wood —
   The fragrant wood and pale:
He planed the broad and feathery coils
   And drove the drastic nail.

28

And from the cedar and the oak—
  The texture of the tree—
He built the House of Time before
  That of Eternity.

How strange to choose a carpenter
  And bind him and impale
Upon the wood he used to work—
  With the beloved nail!

E. MERRILL ROOT

HILLTOPS

No doubt on the hills of Nazareth
  With many another lad
He scrambled, laughing, up the slopes,
  Flushed and young and glad.
How good that he knew love and mirth,
  However brief, until
The years when he must climb—alone—
  A last dark hill.

LESLIE SAVAGE CLARK

JESUS THE CARPENTER

If I could hold within my hand
  The hammer Jesus swung,
Not all the gold in all the land,
Nor jewels countless as the sand,
  All in the balance flung,
Could weigh the value of that thing
Round which his fingers once did cling.

If I could have the table Christ
  Once made in Nazareth,
Not all the pearls in all the sea,
Nor crowns of kings or kings to be
  As long as men have breath,
Could buy that thing of wood he made—
The Lord of Lords who learned a trade.

Yes, but his hammer still is shown
  By honest hands that toil,
And round his table men sit down;
And all are equals, with a crown
  Nor gold nor pearls can soil;
The shop of Nazareth was bare—
But brotherhood was builded there.

CHARLES M. SHELDON

THE HIDDEN YEARS

The hidden years at Nazareth!
  How deep and still they seem,
Like rivers flowing in the dark
  Or waters in a dream!
Like waters under Syrian stars
  Reflecting lights above,
Repeating in their silent depths
  The wonder of God's love!

The hidden years at Nazareth!
　　How clear and true they lie,
As open to the smile of God
　　As to the Syrian sky!
As open to the heart of man
　　As to the genial sun,
With dreams of vast adventuring,
　　And deeds of kindness done!

The hidden years at Nazareth!
　　How radiant they rise,
With life and death in balance laid
　　Before a lad's clear eyes!
O Soul of Youth, forever choose,
　　Forgetting fate or fear,
To live for truth or die with God,
　　Who stands beside thee here!

ALLEN EASTMAN CROSS

The Man Christ Jesus

BREAD

He knew what hunger a man can feel,
  So he broke the fishes and bread
That the weary thousands who followed him
  Might be strengthened and fed.

He knew what hunger a soul can feel,
  Sharing the husks with swine,
So he gave his broken body and blood
  For bread and wine.

LESLIE SAVAGE CLARK

BY THE SEA OF GALILEE

Erect in youthful grace and radiant
  With spirit forces, all imparadised
In a divine compassion, down the slant
  Of these remembering hills he came, the Christ.

KATHARINE LEE BATES

TEMPTED

Into the wilderness
Straightway our Lord was driven of the Spirit;
Swept by that stress
Of rapture, sun and stars were but one shining
Till forty days had passed
And, Son of Man though Son of God, he hungered.

32

Why should he fast
With power to make stones bread; why fear, with succor
Of angels at his call;
Why fail, when all the world was to his Father
A golden ball,
One out of many, but a little present
For a belovèd Son?

Ecstasy, faint with its own bliss, encountered
The scorpion
Of self, love's enemy. For love is holy
In loving; love is safe
Only in saving; love, despised, rejected,
The world's white waif,
Needs nothing that this earth can give of glory,
For love dwelleth in God.

So Christ's immortal rose above his mortal
And on it trod.

KATHARINE LEE BATES

BEACON LIGHT

Whenever I come on kelp-stained nets
    Drying along the sands,
I think of four bronzed fishermen,
    And my heart understands
How joyfully they laid aside
    Their nets by Galilee
To follow one clear Beacon Light
    Across eternity.

LESLIE SAVAGE CLARK

VISION

It is a thread—a tiny, shining thread—
That weaves its way in home, in shop and street;
It skirts the busy paths that know the tread
Of young and dancing, old and tired feet.
Men glimpse its light but dimly, now and then,
As though it beckoned where some lofty track
Leads upward to a dream that might have been—
Above life's deep discouragement and lack.

But One there was who knew the commonplace
Touched with its glory, simple, yet divine.
He saw the yearning soul in every face,
And sensed the dignity of life's design.
Yet, men still dread his vision to embrace—
So poor the upper room, the bread and wine.

IDA NORTON MUNSON

TEMPTATION

They took him to a mountain top to see
Where earth's fair kingdoms flung their golden net
To snare the feet and trick the souls of men.
With slimy craft and cynic guile they said:
If he but sees the glory and the pride,
The pomps and pleasures of this tinsel world,
He will forget his splendid futile dreams.
And so they took him up and tempted him.

They pointed far across their level earth,
East to the fabled empires of the Ind,
Whose rulers' power was as the power of gods,
Where caravans with tinkling camel-bells
Brought silks and perfumes, pearls and ivory,
And tribute from far humbled provinces;
South to the magic kingdom of the Nile,
To Nubia and Abyssinia,
Jungle and desert kingdoms, rude but rich
With slaves and gems and golden yellow sands;
Northward to barbarous lands but dimly seen,
Savage but surging with unmeasured strength;
West where Rome's empire sent her legions forth,
Conquering, building, ruling with wise force,
The mighty mother of an unborn brood
Of nations which should rise and rule the world.

All this they spread before him, tempting him,
And watched to see ambition light his eye,
The lust of power darken his bright face,
And avarice crook his hands to clutch the gold.

But from the mountain peak he raised his eyes,
And saw the deep, calm sky, the stars, and God.

WINFRED ERNEST GARRISON

THE KINGDOM

"Where is the Kingdom?" asked the pompous priest,
Weighted with lore, and spent with fast and feast.
The lowly Christ on his pretension smiled,
And simply said, "In the heart of a little child."

THOMAS CURTIS CLARK

35

ONE THERE WAS

One there was who, passing by,
Touched all life with alchemy;
Grass of field or birds of air
Made his heart of God aware.
Of common salt or smooth-worn yoke
A figure patterned for eager folk;
Of wayside spring or granary
Symbols he made which never die;
From mustard seed or branching vine
Similitudes of things divine.
Meaning to leavening dough he lent;
He made, of bread, a sacrament.

STELLA FISHER BURGESS

COMRADE JESUS

I tramped the pavement, blaming God,
When there beside me Jesus trod.

Now we shall walk, this Friend and I,
Across the earth, the sea, the sky.

I do not know what he may be;
I only know he walks with me.

From Eden barred and Paradise,
Too wisely sad, too sadly wise!

Oh, lonely feet! Oh, bleeding feet
In step with mine on city street!

RALPH CHEYNEY

HANDS OF CHRIST

Hands of Christ,
Divine hands of a carpenter. . . .
I cannot imagine those hands
Forging lances, anviling swords,
Or designing a new model of bomber;
Those hands, hands of Christ,
Were the hands of a carpenter.

Hands of Christ, calloused
Carving cradles,
Shaping plows, building life. . . .
I cannot imagine those hands
Busied with cannon,
Explosive and grenades;
Those calloused hands
Became calloused building life.

Among the feverish hands
That build cruisers
And bombers,
His hands are not found!
His bear the marks of nails,
Heroic marks of sacrifice;
Those hands, bleeding hands,
Strong, steel-nerved hands,
Are the vigorous hands of a carpenter
Quietly building life.

FRANCISCO E. ESTRELLO
(Translated by H. M. Sein)

BLIND BARTIMEUS

Blind Bartimeus at the gates
Of Jericho in darkness waits;
He hears the crowd—he hears a breath
Say, "It is Christ of Nazareth!"
And calls, in tones of agony,
"Jesus, have mercy now on me!"

The thronging multitudes increase;
Blind Bartimeus, hold thy peace!
But still, above the noisy crowd,
The beggar's cry is shrill and loud;
Until they say, "He calleth thee!"
"Fear not, arise, He calleth thee!"

Then saith the Christ, as silent stands
The crowd, "What wilt thou at my hands?"
And he replies, "O give me light!
Rabbi, restore the blind man's sight!"
And Jesus answers, "Go in peace,
Thy faith from blindness gives release!"

Ye that have eyes, yet cannot see,
In darkness and in misery,
Recall those mighty Voices Three,
"Jesus, have mercy now on me!
Fear not, arise, and go in peace!
Thy faith from blindness gives release!"

HENRY WADSWORTH LONGFELLOW

WE WOULD SEE JESUS

We would see Jesus! We would look upon
The light in that divinely human face,
Where lofty majesty and tender grace
  In blended beauty shone.

We would see Jesus, and would hear again
The voice that charmed the thousands by the sea,
Spoke peace to sinners, set the captives free,
  And eased the sufferers' pain.

We would see Jesus, yet not him alone—
But see ourselves as in our Maker's plan;
And in the beauty of the Son of Man
  See man upon his throne.

We would see Jesus, and let him impart
The truth he came among us to reveal,
Till in the gracious message we should feel
  The beating of God's heart.

W. J. SUCKOW

THE MAN CHRIST

He built no temple, yet the farthest sea
Can yield no shore that's barren of His place
  For bended knee.

He wrote no book, and yet His words and prayer
Are intimate on many myriad tongues,
  Are counsel everywhere.

The life He lived has never been assailed,
Nor any precept, as He lived it, yet
  Has ever failed.

He built no kingdom, yet a King from youth
He reigned, is reigning yet; they call His realm
  The kingdom of the Truth.

THERESE LINDSEY

The Way of the Cross

RIDING THROUGH JERUSALEM

I thought it strange he asked for me,
  And bade me carry him,
The noblest one of all the earth,
  Into Jerusalem!

But rumor goes he loved the meek
  And such on him might call,
That may be why he trusted me
  The humblest beast of all.

Yet though he was so great and wise
  Unequaled in his might,
I scarcely knew I bore a King,
  So light he rode—so light!

They sang Hosannah in the streets,
  But I have heard men say
The only time they praised their King
  Was when he rode that day.

Men pushed and shouted all around,
  The air was thick with cries,
They spread their garments at my feet,
  And palms before mine eyes.

They strewed the narrow road with boughs
    And barred my path again—
But the tenderest hand I ever felt
    Was on my bridle chain.

              MARION SUSAN CAMPBELL

WEDNESDAY IN HOLY WEEK

Man's life is death. Yet Christ endured to live
    Preaching and teaching, toiling to and fro,
Few men accepting what he yearned to give,
    Few men with eyes to know
    His face, that Face of Love he stooped to show.

Man's death is life. For Christ endured to die
    In slow unuttered weariness of pain,
A curse and an astonishment, passed by,
    Pointed at, mocked again
    By men for whom he shed his blood—in vain?

             CHRISTINA G. ROSSETTI

THIS IS MY BODY

He saw the Word that spake it,
He took the bread and brake it;
And what that Word did make it,
I do believe and take it.

             JOHN DONNE

"THE LORD TURNED, AND LOOKED UPON PETER"

The Saviour looked on Peter. Aye, no word,
No gesture of reproach! the heavens serene,
Though heavy with armed justice, did not lean
Their thunders that way! the forsaken Lord
Looked only on the traitor. None record
What that look was, none guess: for those who have
    seen
Wronged lovers loving through a death-pang keen,
Or pale-cheeked martyrs smiling to a sword,
Have missed Jehovah at the judgment-call.
And Peter, from the height of blasphemy—
"I never knew this man"—did quail and fall,
As knowing straight that God—and turned free
And went out speechless from the face of all,
And filled the silence, weeping bitterly.

ELIZABETH BARRETT BROWNING

THE FOCUS OF THAT FACE

Peter denied, but Jesus did not scold.
He knew the loneliness, the numbing cold,
The leering jest, the cruel taunting word—
Peter denied him once, and Jesus heard.

Peter denied, but Jesus did not cry
A protest at the oath, or at the lie.
The winds of desolation blew and blew—
Peter denied him twice, and Jesus knew.

43

Thrice he denied; then Jesus broke the trance
With one determined, reassuring glance;
And love was won from terror's dark embrace
Beneath the radiant focus of that Face.

EDWIN MC NEILL POTEAT

THE LONELY CHRIST

The many now had left him, melting fast
    As trembling courtiers from a fallen king;
But were there none beside him at the last
    To whom his love could cling?

Twelve men that night were left; he ate with them
    And pledged the Victor's feast; then led the way
Through moonlit alleys of Jerusalem
    Across the brook to pray.

One he had lost; the others wearied slept;
    With no man by his side the Lord fought on.
They fled into the night; and he was swept
    From court to court alone.

Through solitary ways to peopled lands;
    By desert paths into a city throng;
Silent he went alone, that pilgrim bands
    Might follow him with song.

EDWARD SHILLITO

A BALLAD OF TREES AND THE MASTER

Into the woods my Master went,
    Clean forspent, forspent.
Into the woods my Master came,
    Forspent with love and shame.
But the olives they were not blind to Him,
The little gray leaves were kind to him:
The thorn-tree had a mind to Him
    When into the woods He came.

Out of the woods my Master went,
    And He was well content.
Out of the woods my Master came,
    Content with death and shame.
When Death and Shame would woo Him last,
From under the trees they drew Him last:
'Twas on a tree they slew Him—last
    When out of the woods He came.

SIDNEY LANIER

JUDGE ME, O LORD!

If I had been in Palestine
A poor disciple I had been.
I had not risked or purse or limb
All to forsake, and follow Him.
    But with the vast and wondering throng
    I too had stood and listened long;
    I too had felt my spirit stirred
    When the Beatitudes I heard.

With the glad crowd that sang the psalm,
I too had sung, and strewed the palm;
Then slunk away in dastard shame
When the High Priest denounced His name.
   But when my late companions cried
   "Away! Let Him be crucified!"
   I would have begged, with tremulous
   Pale lips, "Release Him unto us!"

Beside the cross when Mary prayed,
A great way off I too had stayed;
Not even in that hour had dared,
And for my dying Lord declared,
   But beat upon my craven breast,
   And loathed my coward heart, at least,
   To think my life I dared not stake
   And beard the Romans for His sake.

SARAH N. CLEGHORN

SIMON THE CYRENIAN SPEAKS

Look not on me with scorn because
   My skin's of darker hue—
Remember once these shoulders bore
   The cross he bore for you.

GLEN BAKER

GAMBLER

And sitting down they watched him there,
The soldiers did;
There, while they played with dice,
He made his sacrifice,
And died upon the cross to rid
God's world of sin.
He was a gambler, too, my Christ,
He took his life and threw
It for a world redeemed.
And ere his agony was done,
Before the westering sun went down,
Crowning that day with crimson crown,
He knew that he had won.

G. A. STUDDERT-KENNEDY

DEATH OF CHRIST

Pilate made report to Rome,
  Such as seemed worth while;
Sealed it, sent it off to Rome
  With a weary smile.

That was years and years ago—
  When the empire died
On a cross the Romans built
  Out of fear and pride.

ARTHUR R. MACDOUGALL, JR.

SIMON OF CYRENE

I walked that day out to the death-marked hill—
They call the place "the skull"—and saw him bear
His cross until he fell. It was not fair,
I thought, to place it on him. Strength and skill
Were mine from country toil. I bore it till
We came to Golgotha. I did not dare
To speak my grief; I only thought to spare
Him pain—his grateful look lives with me still.

And as we walked along, some women wept.
I could not censure them—my eyes were dim.
But know ye what he said? His words I've kept
Within my heart these years for love of him:
"Weep not for me. Dark days await you too.
Forgive these men: they know not what they do."

GEORGIA HARKNESS

GOOD FRIDAY

Gall is the taste of life when we
Who live must bear our Calvary.
On this day our Master died—
Christ, our Lord, the Crucified.
Upon the cross in agony
He shed his blood for love of me.
In every street, on every hill,
The Heart that stopped is beating still.

VINCENT HOLME

48

E TENEBRIS

Come down, O Christ, and help me! reach thy hand,
For I am drowning in a stormier sea
Than Simon on thy lake of Galilee:
The wine of life is spilt upon the sand,
My heart is as some famine-murdered land
Whence all good things have perished utterly,
And well I know my soul in Hell must lie
If I this night before God's throne should stand.
"He sleeps perchance, or rideth to the chase,
Like Baal, when his prophets howled that name
From morn to noon on Carmel's smitten height."
Nay, peace, I shall behold, before the night,
The feet of brass, the robe more white than flame,
The wounded hands, the weary human face.

OSCAR WILDE

IMMUNITY

Think you to escape
What mortal man can never be without?
What saint upon earth has ever lived apart from
    cross and care?
Why, even Jesus Christ, our Lord, was not even for
    one hour free from his passion's pain.
Christ says, "He needs must suffer,
Rising from the dead,
And enter thus upon his glory."
And how do *you* ask for another road
Than this—the Royal Pathway of the Holy Cross?

THOMAS À KEMPIS

THE MARTYR

And all the while they mocked him and reviled,
And heaped upon him words of infamy;
He stood serenely there, and only smiled
In pity at the blind intensity
Of hate; for well he knew that Love alone
Can cure the ills of men—of nations, too—
Though unregenerate mobs their prophets stone,
And crucify the gentle Christ anew.
So he but smiled, and drained with quiet grace
The bitter cup for lips too eloquent,
And, dauntless, took the soul-degrading place
Designed for thieves—this Prophet heaven-sent!
And when the throng at length had hushed its cry,
Another cross loomed dark against the sky.

NATALIE FLOHR

QUESTION

I wonder if that cypress tree
    Which stood in Eden long ago
And lifted hands where bird and bee
    Winged heaven through the season's flow,
Was ever mindful that a day
    Would bring it aching agony,
And it would stand, a cross, to slay
    The Christ of love on Calvary.

HOWARD MC KINLEY CORNING

FROM "CHRISTUS"

My work is finished; I am strong
In faith, and hope, and charity;
For I have written the things I see,
The things that have been and shall be,
Conscious of right, not fearing wrong;
Because I am in love with Love,
And the sole thing I hate is Hate;
For Hate is death; and Love is life,
A peace, a splendor from above;
And Hate, a never ending strife,
A smoke, a blackness from the abyss
Where unclean serpents coil and hiss!
Love is the Holy Ghost within;
Hate the unpardonable sin!
Who preaches otherwise than this
Betrays his Master with a kiss!

HENRY WADSWORTH LONGFELLOW

SONG

What trees were in Gethsemane,
  What flowers were there to scent,
When Christ for you, and Christ for me,
  Into his garden went?

The fragrant cedar tree was there,
  The lily pale and slim:
They saw his grief, they heard his prayer,
  And wept their dews for him.

And that is why the cedars green
  And why the lilies white
Do whisper of the Master's love
  In gardens, late at night.

CHARLES G. BLANDEN

I HAVE OVERCOME THE WORLD

The crown of empire—must thou yield it now?
(Mine was of thorns they pressed upon My brow.)

Did friends, as foes, desert thee in thy power?
(Mine could not watch with Me one single hour.)

Is all thy life stripped stark through shame and loss?
(Between two thieves I hung upon a cross.)

LAURA SIMMONS

THE GREAT WAGER

How is it proved?
It isn't proved, you fool; it can't be proved.
How can you prove a victory before
It's won? How can you prove a man who leads
To be a leader worth the following,
Unless you follow to the death, and out
Beyond mere death, which is not anything
But Satan's lie upon eternal life?
Well—God's my leader, and I hold that he
Is good, and strong enough to work his plan
And purpose out to its appointed end.

52

I walk in crowded streets, where men
And women, mad with lust, loose-lipped, and lewd,
Go promenading down to hell's wide gates;
Yet have I looked into my mother's eyes
And seen the light that never was on sea
Or land, the light of love, pure love and true,
And on that love I bet my life. . . .

. . . I bet my life on beauty, truth,
And love! not abstract, but incarnate truth;
Not beauty's passing shadow, but its self,
Its very self made flesh—love realized.
I bet my life on Christ, Christ crucified.

G. A. STUDDERT-KENNEDY

CALVARY

Five thousand followed him for fish and loaves,
But only twelve when he broke beauty's bread;
So is it still when a free spirit roves
Over the earth wherever he may tread.
How many blindly worship him who sought
Only for truth and loveliness, who broke
The unjust usages of time, and thought
The rebel thought in him until it spoke!
Yet they who dare a lonely fate—how few
In some Gethsemane beneath the stars,
While the five thousand seek a cushioned pew
And ask for ease, not beauty with its scars!
O You who loved the lilies and the sea,
They have their creed, and You your Calvary.

HUGH ROBERT ORR

The Continuing Calvary

INDIFFERENCE

When Jesus came to Golgotha they hanged Him on
    a tree,
They drave great nails through hands and feet, and
    made a Calvary;
They crowned Him with a crown of thorns, red were
    His wounds and deep,
For those were crude and cruel days, and human
    flesh was cheap.

When Jesus came to Birmingham, they simply passed
    Him by,
They never hurt a hair of Him, they only let Him
    die;
For men had grown more tender, and they would
    not give Him pain,
They only just passed down the street, and left Him
    in the rain.

Still Jesus cried, "Forgive them, for they know not
    what they do,"
And still it rained the winter rain that drenched Him
    through and through;
The crowds went home and left the streets without
    a soul to see,
And Jesus crouched against a wall and cried for
    Calvary.

G. A. STUDDERT-KENNEDY

GOOD FRIDAY

I for thy sake was pierced with heavy sorrow,
   And bore the cross,
Yet heeded not the sharpness of the arrow,
   Nor shame and loss.

So faint not thou, whate'er the burden be,
But bear it bravely, even to Calvary.
                GIROLAMO SAVONAROLA

THE CROSS

Charlemagne carried it far
   Into a pagan fight;
Constantine gilded it like a star
   To glow on the breast of night,
High on an ancient dome,
   Where eyes of tired men turn;
Low on a marble tomb,
   By fading flowers of an urn.

Prelates linked it to a chain,
   The symbol of love, of power—
But only One of us would deign
   To bleed on it for an hour.
Only Christ, of the sons of men,
   Shouldered it for a loss,
Stripped of its glamor scarlet sin,
   And died with it, on a cross.
                RUBY WEYBURN TOBIAS

CRUCIFIXION

Had I been there that cruel day
  When Jesus hung upon the cross,
I would have shouted loud the shame
  And fought with no regard for loss.

But let me think—was it today
  A name was slandered in our town,
When I stood by nor raised a hand
  To put the smooth-tongued liars down?

Had I been there I might have watched
  With mute consent the dark hours through . . .
Forgive me, Lord, for worse than they
  I kill and know well what I do.

CARL S. WEIST

JESUS OF NAZARETH

Would you see the marks of the Roman scourge,
And the pits where the nails were driven?
They are all hidden under fresh wounds.

Much more than forty lashes have I borne since Cal-
    vary;
Blows aimed at striking labor have bruised my body
    sore;
I've known the torture of my kinsmen by the gentile
    mob;
My back is raw from lashings by heroes, masked, at
    night.
Wherever man was beaten, I was whipped.

You see this scar?
　’Twas a bayonet in Flanders.
You see this bruise?
　A slave’s chain pinched me there.
My shoulders stoop?
　Under the heavy load of labor.

You would see the marks of the Roman scourge,
And the pits where the nails were driven?
They are all hidden under fresh wounds.

ERNEST CADMAN COLWELL

FROM "OF OUR LORD'S PASSION"

In Thine hour of holy sadness
Could I share with Thee, what gladness
Should Thy cross to me be showing.
Gladness past all thought of knowing,
　Bowed beneath Thy cross to die!

Blessed Jesus, thanks I render
That in bitter death, so tender,
Thou dost hear Thy suppliant calling;
Save me, Lord, and keep from falling
　From Thee, when mine hour is nigh.

BERNARD OF CLAIRVAUX

ALL TOO SLOWLY

Like a glacier man advances.
　　All too slowly does he learn,
Fighting once with spears and lances,
　　Now with bombs that blast and burn.

Must he keep forever trying
　　To annihilate the race?
Must he keep on crucifying
　　Christ in field and market place?

All too slowly, like a glacier
　　Man goes on through fog and hate.
May he find the one, the holy
　　Way of love before too late!

LUCIA TRENT

THE JEW TO JESUS

O Man of my own people, I alone
Among these alien ones can know thy face,
I who have felt the kinship of our race
Burn in me as I sit where they intone
Thy praises,—those who, striving to make known
A God for sacrifice, have missed the grace
Of thy sweet human meaning in its place,
Thou who art of our blood-bond and our own.

Are we not sharers of thy Passion? Yea,
In spirit-anguish closely by thy side
We have drained the bitter cup, and, tortured, felt
With thee the bruising of each heavy welt.
In every land is our Gethsemane.
A thousand times have we been crucified.

FLORENCE KIPER FRANK

IF HE SHOULD COME

If he should come tomorrow, the Meek and Lowly
    One,
To walk familiar pathways beneath an older sun,
What king would hail his coming, what seer proclaim
    his birth,
If he should come tomorrow, would he find faith on
    earth?

If he should come tomorrow, what marvels would he
    see?
White wings that soar the heavens, great ships that
    sail the sea,
A million spires arising to praise his holy name,
But human hearts unchastened, and human greed
    the same.

As in the days of Herod, the money-changers still
In God's own House contriving against the Father's
    will;
His messengers in exile, corruption on the throne,
And all the little company disbanded and alone.

Oh, let him come in glory with all the powers of God,
Begirt with shining legions to rule with iron rod,
Till greed be purged forever from out the souls of
    men;
Lest he who comes tomorrow be crucified again!

LILITH LORRAINE

Resurrection

RESURRECTION

It came so quietly—the first gray light,
That touched the open tomb that Easter dawn,
Long years ago. There, where the weight of night
And death had lain a dark despair upon
Each sorrowing heart, came morning, a bird's voice,
And cypress trees showed sunrise trickling through.
The day that bade the whole wide world rejoice
Was born where lilies in a garden grew.

It will come quietly. There will be bread,
Water for long-parched lips. The hurt-filled breast
Will sense a healing comfort, void of dread.
Slowly earth's war-torn peoples will have rest
And, with its life, its light, its sweet release,
Like that first Easter morning, will come peace.

IDA NORTON MUNSON

HOPE

He died!
And with him perished all that men hold dear;
Hope lay beside him in the sepulcher,
Love grew corse cold, and all things beautiful beside
    Died when he died.

61

He rose!
And with him hope arose, and life and light.
Men said, "Not Christ but Death died yesternight."
And joy and truth and all things virtuous
   Rose when he rose.

ANONYMOUS

EASTER MESSAGE

Almost two thousand years ago today
The stone upon His grave was rolled away,
And in the blinding darkness of the tomb
He rose and shattered there the grief and gloom
Within the hearts of those who worshiped Him.
Although that day and time have now grown dim,
One message through the ages has been hurled:
His love is hope and light for all the world.
And as the dawn of Easter fills the skies
We, too, with Him in spirit must arise;
For even underneath us in the earth
There is a faithful promise of rebirth.
If there's a stone against your heart today,
Look up to Him and it will roll away.

JOHN VAN BRAKLE

EASTER

Lord, now that Spring is in the world,
  And every tulip is a cup
Filled with the wine of Thy great love,
  Lift Thou me up.

Raise Thou my heart as flowers arise
  To greet the glory of Thy day,
With soul as clean as lilies are,
  And white as they.

Let me not fear the darkness now,
  Since Life and Light break through Thy tomb;
Teach me that doubts no more oppress,
  No more consume.

Show me that Thou art April, Lord,
  And Thou the flowers and the grass;
Then, when awake the soft spring winds,
  I'll hear Thee pass!

CHARLES HANSON TOWNE

"IF A MAN DIE, SHALL HE LIVE AGAIN?"

> I will repudiate the lie
> Men tell of life;
> How it will pass
> As fragile flower, or butterfly,
> Whose dust shall nourish
> April grass.
>
> Since One, for love, died on a tree
> And in the stony
> Tomb was lain,
> Behold I show a mystery:
> All sepulchres
> Are sealed in vain!

JOHN RICHARD MORELAND

HE IS RISEN

The Lord indeed is risen
From out his earthly prison,
And now, all kings above,
He reigns forevermore—
The Lord of Life, the King of Love,
Life's loving Conqueror.

JOHN OXENHAM

FROM "EASTER HYMN"
(*In "Faust"*)

Christ is arisen,
  Joy to thee, mortal!
Out of his prison,
  Forth from its portal!
Christ is not sleeping,
  Seek him no longer;
Strong was his keeping,
  Jesus was stronger.

Christ is arisen,
  Seek him not here;
Lonely his prison,
  Empty his bier;
Vain his entombing,
  Spices and lawn,
Vain the perfuming,
  Jesus is gone.

Christ is arisen,
    Joy to thee, mortal!
Empty his prison,
    Broken his portal!
Rising, he giveth
    His shroud to the sod;
Risen, he liveth,
    And liveth to God.

J. W. VON GOETHE

RESURRECTION

In this brown seed, so dry and hard,
I see a flower in my door yard.
You, chrysalis in winding sheet,
Are butterfly all dainty sweet.
All life is warmed by spring's sweet breath,
And Christ our Lord has conquered death.

AGNES W. STORER

EASTER JOY

I, too, O Christ, denied you,
    And felt the dawn-winds blow
Cold and gray upon my cheek,
    And heard the cock's loud crow;

I, too, sat silent while the scribes
    With cynic wisdom tried,
Buffeted, reviled and mocked,
    Condemned you—crucified.

But I have seen the dead arise,
    The spring wake fair and strong;
And doubt has changed to soaring faith,
    Despair to love and song.

DAISY CONWAY PRICE

FROM "CHRISTMAS EVE"

Earth breaks up, time drops away,
In flows heaven, with its new day
Of endless life, when he who trod,
Very Man and Very God,
This Earth in weakness, shame and pain,
Dying the death whose signs remain
Up yonder on the accursèd tree—
Shall come again, no more to be
Of Captivity the thrall,
But the One God, all in all,
King of Kings and Lord of Lords,
As his servant John received the words,
"I died, and live forevermore!"

ROBERT BROWNING

THE SEPULCHER IN THE GARDEN

What though the Flowers in Joseph's Garden grew
Of rarest perfume and of fairest hue,
That morn when Magdalene hastened through
    Its fragrant, silent paths?

She caught no scent of budding almond tree;
Her eyes, tear-blinded still from Calvary,
Saw neither lily nor anemone—
   Naught save the Sepulcher.

But when the Master whispered "Mary," lo!
The Tomb was hid; the Garden all ablow;
And burst in bloom the Rose of Jericho—
   From that day "Mary's Flower."

JOHN FINLEY

EASTER CAROL

O Earth! throughout thy borders
   Re-don thy fairest dress;
And everywhere, O Nature,
   Throb with new happiness;
Once more to new creation
   Awake, and death gainsay,
For death is swallowed up of life,
   And Christ is risen today.

Let peals of jubilation
   Ring out in all the lands;
With hearts of deep elation
   Let sea with sea clasp hands;
Let one supreme Te Deum
   Roll round the world's highway,
For death is swallowed up of life,
   And Christ is risen today.

GEORGE NEWELL LOVEJOY

RESURRECTION

If it be all for nought, for nothingness
At last, why does God make the world so fair?
Why spill this golden splendor out across
The western hills, and light the silver lamp
Of eve? Why give me eyes to see, the soul
To love so strong and deep? Then, with a pang
This brightness stabs me through, and wakes within
Rebellious voice to cry against all death?
Why set this hunger for eternity
To gnaw my heartstrings through, if death ends all?
If death ends all, then evil must be good,
Wrong must be right, and beauty ugliness.
God is a Judas who betrays his Son
And, with a kiss, damns all the world to hell—
If Christ rose not again.

UNKNOWN SOLDIER, *killed in World War 1*

CHRIST HAS RISEN

Christ has risen—else in vain
All the sunshine, all the rain,
All the warmth and quickening,
And renewal of the spring.
Vain they were to charm our eyes,
Greening earth and gracious skies,
Growth and beauty, bud or bloom,
If within their fast-sealed tomb
All our dearer dead must dwell,
Sharing not the miracle.

Crocus tips in shining row,
Welcome, for your sign we know.
Every bud on every bough
Has its message for us now,
Since the Lord on Easter Day
Burst the bonds of prisoning clay;
All the springtime has a voice,
Every heart may dare rejoice,
Every grave, no more a prison,
Joins the chorus, "Christ is risen."

SUSAN COOLIDGE

EASTER

Today unnumbered church bells ring.
  Unnumbered hands are clasped in prayer
To Him who suffered, lived, and died,
  And rose from sorrow and despair.

This is the season for rebirth
  Of human hope and joy and love,
When beauty blooms again on earth
  And brighter glows the sky above.

The cold things in this changing world
  Have no place in your heart today,
For even Winter's icy shroud
  Has long since thawed and flowed away.

So listen as the church bells ring
  And clasp your hands again in prayer,
Then joyfully arise and sing;
  His love will conquer your despair.

JOHN VAN BRAKLE

Come, Follow Me

WHAT IS IT JESUS SAITH?

What is it Jesus saith unto the soul?
"Take up the cross, and come and follow Me."
One word he saith to all men: none may be
Without a cross yet hope to reach the goal.
Then heave it bravely up, and brace thy whole
Body to bear: it will not weigh on thee
Past strength; or if it crush thee to thy knee
Take heart of grace, for grave shall be thy dole.

Give thanks today, and let tomorrow take
Heed to itself; today imports thee more.
Tomorrow may not dawn like yesterday:
Until that unknown tomorrow go thy way,
Suffer and work and strive for Jesus' sake—
Who tells thee what tomorrow keeps in store?

CHRISTINA G. ROSSETTI

"LOVE SUFFERETH LONG"

The Writ of Loving Well
   Still makes its old demands:
A sometime residence in Hell,
   The nailprints in the hands.

All those who pledge themselves,
    And to its terms agree,
Must chance an unexclusive cross,
    A common Calvary!

SARA HENDERSON HAY

SACRAMENT

There lies no magic in this bit of bread,
    No charm to save me in this sip of wine.
No food can nourish if the soul be dead,
    No lifeless heart respond to fire divine.

Here at God's altar I may kneel in vain
    Unless I glow with love, selfless and deep.
When I do truly serve my fellow men
    The Eucharist I keep.

UNA W. HARSEN

FOLLOW ME

Lord, I would follow, but—
First, I would see what means that wondrous call
That peals so sweetly through Life's rainbow hall,
That thrills my heart with quivering golden chords,
And fills my soul with joys seraphical.

Lord, I would follow, but—
First, I would leave things straight before I go,—
Collect my dues, and pay the debts I owe;
Lest when I'm gone, and none is here to tend,
Time's ruthless hand my garnering o'erthrow.

Lord, I would follow, but—
First, I would see the end of this high road
That stretches straight before me, fair and broad;
So clear the way I cannot go astray,
It surely leads me equally to God.

Lord, I would follow,—yea,
Follow I *will*,—but first so much there is
That claims me in life's vast emergencies,—
Wrongs to be righted, great things to be done;
Shall I neglect these vital urgencies?

Who answers Christ's insistent call
Must give himself, his life, his all,
Without one backward look.
Who sets his hand unto the plow,
And glances back with anxious brow,
His calling hath mistook.
Christ claims him wholly for his own;
He must be Christ's, and Christ's alone.

JOHN OXENHAM

THY KINGDOM COME!

O Christ, great Lover of all souls,
    Meek Lord of sympathy,
Our lips, how eloquent they are!
    Our hearts, how far from Thee!

We worship our dividing walls,
    We boast our caste and clan;
Oh, let Thy Kingdom quickly come—
    A brotherhood of man.

If any churchly fashions lurk
  To thwart Thy larger will,
Let them in love be crucified
  As we Thy wish fulfill.

Renew in us "good will to men,"
  Transform our selfish creeds,
That we may pray "Thy Kingdom come"
  In eloquence of deeds.

THOMAS CURTIS CLARK

A PRAYER FOR CHRISTIAN UNITY

O Master of the Galilean Way,
Forgive us for the vows we fail to keep:
Forgive us that we so neglect Thy sheep,
So idly waste this shining harvest day!
Forgive us for the stumblingblocks we lay
Along the paths by which men seek Thee! Sweep
From our small minds the strife that holds Thee
    cheap!
Break Thou the bread of life with us, we pray!

What matter if we cannot understand
The mystery of Love that is divine,
Nor pierce the veil! Dear Lord, our faith increase
To know that, since our hands may reach Thy hand,
Our lives are made all-powerful, through Thine,
To heal a wounded world and bring it peace!

MOLLY ANDERSON HALEY

FROM "GARETH AND LYNETTE"
(*In "Idylls of the King"*)

Man am I grown, a man's work must I do.
Follow the deer? follow the Christ, the King,
Live pure, speak true, right wrong, follow the King—
Else, wherefore born?

ALFRED TENNYSON

FROM "BEFORE"

Our wars are wars of life, and wounds of love,
With intellect spears and long-winged arrows of
    thought,
Mutual, in one another's wrath, all renewing
We live as One Man. For contracting our infinite
    senses
We behold multitude; or expanding, we behold as
    One,
As one man all the Universal Family; and that man
We call Jesus the Christ, and he is us, and we in him,
Live in perfect harmony in Eden the land of life,
Giving, receiving, and forgiving each other's tres-
    passes.

ROBERT BROWNING

The Continuing Christ

THE CONTINUING CHRIST

Far, far away is Bethlehem,
    And years are long and dim,
Since Mary held the Holy Child
    And angels sang for Him.
But still to hearts where love and faith
    Make room for Christ in them,
He comes again, the Child from God,
    To find His Bethlehem.

Beyond the sea is Galilee
    And ways which Jesus trod,
And hidden there are those high hills
    Where He communed with God;
Yet on the plains of common life,
    Through all the world of men,
The voice that once said, "Follow me,"
    Speaks to our hearts again.

Gethsemane and Calvary
    And death and bitter loss,
Are these but echoes drifting down
    From a forgotten cross?
Nay, Lord, for all our living sins
    Thy cross is lifted up,
And as of old we hear Thee say,
    "Can ye, too, drink My cup?"

O Life that seems so long ago,
    And yet is ever new,
The fellowship of love with Thee,
    Through all the years is true.
O Master over death and time,
    Reveal Thyself, we pray,
And as before amongst Thine own,
    Dwell Thou in us today!

W. RUSSELL BOWIE

THE FAITH OF CHRIST'S FREEMEN

Our faith is in the Christ who walks
    With men today, in street and mart;
The constant Friend who thinks and talks
    With those who seek him with the heart.

His gospel calls for living men
    With singing blood and minds alert;
Strong men, who fall to rise again,
    Who strive and bleed, with courage girt.

We serve no God whose work is done,
    Who rests within his firmament:
Our God, his labors but begun,
    Toils evermore, with power unspent.

God was and is and e'er shall be;
    Christ lived and loved—and loves us still;
And man goes forward, proud and free,
    God's present purpose to fulfill.

THOMAS CURTIS CLARK

FROM "THE MAY QUEEN"

He taught me all the mercy, for he show'd me all
    the sin.
Now, tho' my lamp was lighted late, there's One will
    let me in.

ALFRED TENNYSON

FAITH

I did not see the crown
He wore,
Nor touched the wounds
Of One who died,
Nor saw the rock that sealed
The door,
Nor comforted the ones
Who cried.

Yet, I believe Christ lives,
Although
I never found
The empty tomb;
Even today he lives,
I know. . . .
I saw a shadow
In my room.

DONALD EARL EDWARDS

COME UNTO ME

We labor and are heavy-laden. Where
Shall we find rest unto our souls? We bleed
On thorn and flint, and rove in pilgrim weed
From shrine to shrine, but comfort is not there.
What went we out into thy desert bare,
O Human Life, to see? Thy greenest reed
Is Love, unmighty for our utmost need,
And shaken with the wind of our despair.
A voice from Heaven like dew on Hermon falleth,
That voice whose passion paled the olive leaf
In thy dusky aisles, Gethsemane, thou blest
Of gardens. 'Tis the Man of Sorrows calleth,
The Man of Sorrows and acquaint with grief:
"Come unto Me, and I will give you rest."

KATHARINE LEE BATES

IN PALESTINE

Have the rocks on the hillside voices—
    And the clods under trampling feet?
Do the cobblestones utter a message,
    And the pebbles tell secrets sweet?

Yes, the hills and the vales have voices,
    The rocks by the wayside speak:
They tell of the march of the ages,
    And of Him whom the nations seek.

GEORGE W. CARLIN

BENEATH SUCH RAINS

The day I rode through Devonshire
　　The lonely downs were dark with rain,
And all the Dorset fields a blur
　　Of dripping hedge and dreary lane.

The sea was very near. The air
　　Was damp and from a shifting sky.
Only one thing was lovely there
　　And good to travelers going by.

The purple patches of the heather
　　Held me like song, and I would go
Through all the dull and weary weather
　　Thinking Who might have seen them so,

Thinking Who might have come this way
　　With laughing breath and splashing hurry
Beneath such rains, on such a day
　　To reach his hut at Glastonbury.

JAMES E. WARREN, JR.

[*Note: According to an old legend, Jesus, as a boy, visited England with Joseph of Arimathea, who was a merchant. Christ built a hut at Glastonbury, and, after the crucifixion, it was to this spot that Joseph brought what was to be called the Holy Grail.*]

CHRIST CAN GIVE THEE HEART

But Christ can give thee heart who loveth thee:
Can set thee in the eternal ecstasy
Of his great jubilee:
Can give thee dancing heart and shining face,
And lips filled full of grace,
And pleasures of the rivers and the sea.
Who knocketh at his door
He welcomes evermore:
Kneel down before
That ever-open door
(The time is short) and smite
Thy breast, and pray with all thy might.

CHRISTINA G. ROSSETTI

FAITH

Religion is of faith indeed,
    In God and life and Jesus Christ—
I wrote my name unto this creed,
    And still my need went unsufficed.

But when I turned aside from prayer
    To make another's need my own,
Lo! Christ and God were standing there,
    And Faith stood up in flesh and bone.

HUGH O. ISBELL

TO HIM WHO WALKS THE WATER

We sink within this earth's dark waters: we
Sink, human, in our deeper Galilee;
Alone, we drown within that bitter wave
Where very life itself becomes our grave.
Then Christ, who walks the waters as the land,
Touches our faltering hand with his firm hand—
And lo! we walk upon the drifting sea
Of time, made steadfast with eternity.
To Thee, O Christ, Thy drowning creatures cry:
"O save us from the lives by which we die!"

E. MERRILL ROOT

IN THE WAY OF PEACE

Jesus, whose love rekindles dying fires
    Flickering to ashes in our aching hearts,
Be Thou the goal of all our best desires,
    The dawn from which our longing ne'er departs.

When night's grim loneliness throbs like a wound
    And day's bright sunshine stabs us like a sword,
Us, with Thy peace, like traveler's cloak, around,
    Enfold as we go forward, O our Lord.

Through the sharp thorns that lie along our way
    Make Thou a path for tired and bleeding feet,
And bring us to the wonder of that day
    When Love and Memory in Thee shall meet.

LAUCHLAN MAC LEAN WATT

A RIVER OF GRACE

Make of my heart an upper room, I pray,
　　Swept clean of pride, let self be but a door
Through which young lives may come to Thee this
　　　day
　　To know Thee as they have not known before.

Speak through my voice that they may hear Thine
　　　own.
　　Shine through my life in beauty and in truth
That they may see the Comrade Christ alone
　　And in the glad impulsiveness of youth

Rise up as did those fisher lads of Thine
　　Who left their boats and nets to follow Thee,
So may they walk beside Thee, these of mine
　　Whom out of all the world "Thou gavest me."

MOLLY ANDERSON HALEY

THE TRUE GIFT

I gave a beggar from my scanty store
Of hard-earned gold. He spent the shining ore
And came again, and yet again, still cold
And hungry, as before.

I gave the Christ, and through that Christ of mine
He found himself, a man, supreme, divine,
　　Fed, clothed, and crowned with blessings manifold,
And now he begs no more.

ANONYMOUS

THE CARPENTER OF GALILEE

The Carpenter of Galilee
  Comes down the street again,
In every land, in every age,
  He still is building men.

On Christmas Eve we hear him knock;
  He goes from door to door:
"Are any workmen out of work?
  The Carpenter needs more."

HILDA W. SMITH

THE RHYTHM OF HIS LIFE

Until I caught the rhythm of his life,
  I had not heard the music of the spheres,
The simple cadences of ancient psalms,
  The lyric beauty of a thousand years.

I had not seen the loveliness of dawn
  Across the lifted hills, the gold and gray
Of winter sunsets, or the moonlight's hush
  Upon a sleeping world, or flash of spray

Against eternal rocks! And now, behold!
  The Voiceless Future is a singing flame!
White Presences attend me everywhere,
  Their canticles an echo of his name!

MARY HALLET

PRAYER

Bear with me, Master, when I turn from Thee.
Pity me in my loss.
Forgive me, knowing I shall come again
As certainly as day that follows night.
Steel magnetized will ever seek the pole,
So I, of my free will which is not free,
But in its very nature bent to Thine,
Will come to rest in Thee.
I, the swinging needle in the compass of the world;
Thou, the perpetual North.

EDITH LOVEJOY PIERCE

A PRAYER FOR THE PRESENCE OF CHRIST

Reveal Thy Presence now, O Lord,
   As in the Upper Room of old;
Break Thou our bread, grace Thou our board,
   And keep our hearts from growing cold.

THOMAS TIPLADY

THOU LIGHT OF AGES

Thou Light of Ages, Source of living truth,
   Shine into every groping, seeking mind;
Let plodding age and pioneering youth
   Each day some clearer, brighter pathway find.

Thou Light of Ages, shining forth in Christ,
  Whose brightness darkest ages could not dim,
Grant us the spirit which for him sufficed—
  Rekindle here the torch of love for him.
ROLLAND W. SCHLOERB

CHRISTMAS BELLS

I heard the bells on Christmas day
Their old familiar carols play,
  And wild and sweet
  The word repeat,
Of "Peace on earth, good will to men!"

And thought how, as the day had come,
The belfries of all Christendom
  Had rolled along
  The unbroken song,
Of "Peace on earth, good will to men!"

Till ringing, singing on its way,
The world revolved from night to day,—
  A voice, a chime,
  A chant sublime,
Of "Peace on earth, good will to men!"

.   .   .   .

Then pealed the bells more loud and deep;
"God is not dead; nor doth he sleep!
  The wrong shall fail,
  The right prevail,
With peace on earth, good will to men!"
HENRY WADSWORTH LONGFELLOW

FROM "ABIDE IN ME"

The soul alone, like a neglected harp,
   Grows out of tune, and needs that Hand divine;
Dwell Thou within it! tune and touch the chord,
   Till every note and string shall answer Thine!

Abide in me,—There have been moments pure
   When I have seen Thy face and felt Thy power;
Then evil lost its grasp, and passion, hushed,
   Owned the divine enchantment of the hour.

HARRIET BEECHER STOWE

PRAYER HYMN

Lord of all pots and pans and things, since I've no
      time to be
A Saint by doing lovely things, or watching late with
      Thee,
Or dreaming in the dawnlight, or storming Heaven's
      gates,
Make me a saint by getting meals, and washing up
      the plates.

Although I must have Martha's hands, I have a Mary
      mind;
And when I black the boots and shoes, Thy sandals,
      Lord, I find.
I think of how they trod the earth, what time I scrub
      the floor;
Accept this meditation, Lord, I haven't time for
      more.

Warm all the kitchen with Thy love, and light it
    with Thy peace;
Forgive me all my worrying, and make all grumbling
    cease.
Thou who didst love to give men food, in room, or
    by the sea,
Accept this service that I do—I do it unto Thee.

M. K. H.

JESUS OF NAZARETH PASSES BY

Unshaken by the storms that rage
  O'er all the earth, in every time,
Moves one lone Man through every age,
  Serene, invincible, sublime.
Through all the centuries he goes,
  His timeless journey to complete,
Divinely calm, as one who knows
  The way is sure beneath his feet.

Wild storms of hate beat round his head,
  Earth rocks beneath the crash of war,
But still, with smooth, unhurried tread,
  He moves, untroubled as before.
Over the wrecks of fallen states,
  Through fair, proud nations yet to fall,
Passes the Master of their fates,
  The silent Sovereign of them all.

Unfaltering through the darkest night,
    Denied by man, though loving man,
His face gives back the morning light,
    His calm eyes see God's finished plan.
One little troubled day we bide,
    And then find rest in beds of clay;
But our brief day is glorified—
    We have seen Jesus pass this way.

GEORGE T. LIDDELL

FAITH

It is the road, the chart,
The wafer and the wine;
Who lives by faith
Shall find life good
And clutch the things divine.

Christ and his word shall be
Their sustenance till breath
Slips from the clay—
Who lives by faith
Shall never taste of death.

JOHN RICHARD MORELAND

The Revolutionist

UPON THIS ROCK

O Carpenter of Nazareth,
Of lowliest birth, of bitterest death,
A workman, and the workman's friend,
When will the worker's Calvary end?

Thou who art named the Prince of Peace,
When will the reign of Caesars cease?
When will the warring legions pass,
And all the strife of caste and class?

They call Thee God, but make Thee fool
Who laud the soul and damn the tool;
Who make Thee sovereign of the skies
But build Thee here a House of Lies.

When men are labor-born today,
Where labor walks Golgotha's way,
Where workmen share Thy workman's smock—
Where else Thy Church, who else Thy Rock?

All other Rocks have proven sand;
All other Churches fouled Thy hand.
Thy fellow workers of the earth
Are come to give Thy Kingdom birth.

ROBERT WHITAKER

THE CHRIST MILITANT

We serve no weak and timid Christ,
   We would not heed a futile Lord;
The man we follow unto death
   Was not afraid of rod or sword.

He asked no pillow for his head,
   He sought no luxury of ease;
The tides that swept his daring soul
   Were dauntless as the mighty seas.

The little town of Nazareth
   Could never bound his spirit's aim;
He dreamed that every zone of earth
   Should know the wonder of his name.

A soldier of the truth was he;
   His anger flamed at vested wrong;
He challenged kings to fateful war,
   And sounded clear his battle song.

Against the cruel lords of pride
   He stood a warrior, strong and sure,
And whipped the greedy temple thieves
   Who sought to cheat his helpless poor.

He ruled the stubborn hearts of men,
   And yet disdained the tyrant's rod—
The mighty Captain of the Right,
   The Saviour of the World of God.

THOMAS CURTIS CLARK

TO A REVOLUTIONIST

With deadly drive Your grim advance
Against tradition swept the world.
But we have found a way to conquer even You.
We talk like rebels, deprecate tradition,
Discuss with unchanged hearts a world of change,
And make of You, tradition-smashing Christ,
Another dead tradition!

HAROLD E. FEY

FROM "THE TOILING OF FELIX"

Never in a costly palace did I rest on golden bed,
Never in a hermit's cavern have I eaten idle bread.

Born within a lowly stable where the cattle round
  Me stood,
Trained a carpenter of Nazareth, I have toiled and
  found it good.

They who tread the path of labor follow where My
  feet have trod;
They who work without complaining do the Holy
  Will of God.

Where the many toil together, there am I among
  My own;
When the tired workman sleepeth, then am I with
  him alone.

I, the Peace that passeth knowledge, dwell amid the
daily strife,
I, the Bread of Heaven, am broken in the sacrament
of life.

HENRY VAN DYKE

UNEMPLOYED

"It's hard to be without a wage," I said,
"It's worse to not be wanted, your work unpriced."
"I know too well," the man in the line ahead
Spoke up. "And who are you?" "They call me
Christ."

RALPH CHEYNEY

HIS THRONE IS WITH THE OUTCAST

I followed where they led,
And in a hovel rude,
With naught to fence the weather from his head,
The King I sought for meekly stood;
A naked hungry child
Clung round his gracious knee,
And a poor hunted slave looked up and smiled
To bless the smile that set him free;
New miracles I saw his presence do,
No more I knew the hovel bare and poor,
The gathered chips into a woodpile grew
The broken morsel swelled to goodly store.
I knelt and wept: my Christ no more I seek.
His throne is with the outcast and the weak.

JAMES RUSSELL LOWELL

FROM "THE VISION OF SIR LAUNFAL"

And the voice that was calmer than silence said,
"Lo it is I, be not afraid!
In many climes, without avail,
Thou hast spent thy life for the Holy Grail;
Behold, it is here—this cup which thou
Didst fill at the streamlet for me but now;
This crust is my body broken for thee,
This water His blood that died on the tree;
The Holy Supper is kept, indeed,
In whatso we share with another's need,—
Not that which we give, but what we share,—
For the gift without the giver is bare;
Who gives himself with his alms feeds three,
Himself, his hungering neighbor, and me."

JAMES RUSSELL LOWELL

MASTER SURGEON

Men at the Council Tables,
The map of the world lies before you
Like a broken body.
You are the surgeons in consultation,
Stroking your beards,
Tapping your fingers.
Sharp words are shot from your lips,
Angry gestures flung from your hands.

The broken body tosses while you quarrel,
The broken body moans while you wrangle.

There is only One Surgeon who can heal.
His eyes are wide with compassion.
His mouth is soft with sympathy.
His hands . . . Look! Are they not spiked with nails?
He stands at your sides ready with his healing.
Seek him out and listen, men at the Council Tables,
For only his wisdom can heal
The broken, moaning body of the world.

LUCIA TRENT

JESUS

Jesus, whose lot with us was cast,
Who saw it out, from first to last;
Patient and fearless, tender, true,
Carpenter, vagabond, felon, Jew;
Whose humorous eye took in each phase
Of full, rich life this world displays
Yet evermore kept fast in view
The far-off goal it leads us to;
Who, as your hour neared, did not fail—
The world's fate trembling in the scale—
With your half-hearted band to dine,
And chat across the bread and wine;
Then went out firm to face the end,
Alone, without a single friend;
Who felt, as your last words confessed,
Wrung from a proud, unflinching breast
By hours of dull, ignoble pain,
Your whole life's fight was fought in vain—
Would I could win and keep and feel
That heart of love, that spirit of steel!

ANONYMOUS

JESUS

The martyred Christ of the working class, the in-
spired evangel of the downtrodden masses, the
world's supreme revolutionary leader,
Whose love for the poor and the children of the poor
hallowed all the days of his consecrated life,
lighted up and made forever holy the dark
tragedy of his death, and gave to the ages his
divine inspiration and his deathless name.

EUGENE V. DEBS

WHAT OUR LORD WROTE IN THE DUST

We have saved the soul of the man who killed,
  We have turned to shrive the thief;
We restored the pride of the man who lied
  And we gave him our belief;
But for her who fell we have fashioned hell
  With a faith all stern and just—
It was so of old; and no man hath told
  What our Lord wrote in the dust.

We have sighed betimes for our brothers' crimes
  And have bade them be of cheer,
For the flesh is weak, and the soul grown meek
  May yet read its title clear.
But we draw away from the one astray
  As the truly righteous must,
She is cursed indeed—and we did not read
  What our Lord wrote in the dust.

For the men who thieved, and who killed and lied—
    Who have slain the woman's soul—
We have worked and prayed, and have seen them
      made
    All clean and pure and whole,
But we drive her out with a righteous shout
    In our Pharisaic trust,
So the man goes free—but we do not see
    What our Lord wrote in the dust.

ANONYMOUS

NOT MADE WITH HANDS

Carpenter, what are you building now?
    Have your still hands lost their art?
I am building a house not made with hands
    Eternal in the heart.

Carpenter, what are you seeing now,
    With your hammers lying still?
I see the temples of freedom rise,
    Sheer from the rock of will.

Carpenter, what are you saying now?
    Is it drowned in the planet's spin?
No sound can drown what the Chosen hear;
    I am calling my Builders in.

I am calling the meek to inherit the earth,
    I am trampling the serpent's spawn,
I am hewing the beams for the Ark of Peace
    That will sail in the Golden Dawn.

LILITH LORRAINE

The Lost Christ

HE—THEY—WE

They hailed him King as they passed by,
    They strewed their garments in the road,
But they were set on earthly things,
    And he on God.

They sang his praise for that he did,
    But gave his message little thought;
They could not see that their soul's good
    Was all he sought.

They could not understand why he,
    With powers so vast at his command,
Should hesitate to claim their rights
    And free the land.

Their own concern and this world's hopes
    Shut out the wonder of his News;
And we, with larger knowledge, still
    His Way refuse.

He walks among us still, unseen,
    And still points out the only way,
But we still follow other gods
    And him betray.

                                    JOHN OXENHAM

THE LOST CHRIST

Where have we laid him now,
This Christ we once so sadly
    placed within a tomb?
So often we have buried him
    safely stowed away, where
    we could come to worship
    and anoint!
We have wrapped him in the trappings
    of the altar,
    and rolled the stone of creed
    against his tomb.
We have dug his grave in busyness
    and repeatedly interred him
    in committee. . . .
But always, when we look to find him
    where we laid him,
    the voice of faith proclaims:
    "He is not here. He is risen.
    He goeth before you!"

FRANKLIN D. ELMER, JR.

THE IMAGE IN THE FORUM

Not Baal, but Christus-Jingo! Heir
    Of him who once was crucified!
The red stigmata still are there,
    The crimson spear-wounds in the side;
But raised aloft as God and Lord,
He holds the Money-bag and Sword.

See, underneath the Crown of Thorn,
   The eye-balls fierce, the features grim!
And merrily from night to morn
   We chant his praise and worship him—
Great Christus-Jingo, at whose feet
Christian and Jew and Atheist meet!

A wondrous god! most fit for those
   Who cheat on change, then creep to prayer;
Blood on his heavenly altar flows,
   Hell's burning incense fills the air,
And Death attests in street and lane
The hideous glory of his reign.

O gentle Jew, from age to age
   Walking the waves Thou could'st not tame,
This god hath ta'en Thy heritage,
   And stolen Thy sweet and stainless Name!
To him we crawl and bend the knee,
Naming Thy Name, but scorning Thee!

ROBERT BUCHANAN

THE JERICHO ROAD

I know the road to Jericho,
   It's in a part of town
That's full of factories and filth.
   I've seen the folk go down,

Small folk with roses in their cheeks
   And starlight in their eyes,
And seen them fall among the thieves,
   And heard their helpless cries

99

When toiling took their roses red
    And robbed them of their stars
And left them pale and almost dead.
    The while, in motor-cars

The priests and levites speeding by
    Read of the latest crimes
In headlines spread in black or red
    Across the "Evening Times."

How hard for those in limousines
    To heal the hurt of man!
It was a slow-paced ass that bore
    The Good Samaritan.

                    EDWIN MC NEILL POTEAT

BY AN ANCIENT SEA

Here, on this sunny shore, in simpler days
A Wise Man walked, communing with his friends.
He loved these quiet waters, and the flowers
That flecked those fields with blue and gold. What
        hours
Of thoughtful talk were theirs—of him who sends
Earth's summer beauty; of the varied ways
Of human life; and of the life to be.
They understood his words—those simple men;
No futile argument or sophistry
Ensnared and vexed their minds. Oh, that again
This Man might talk to us, and know our needs!
Alas, his voice is drowned by jangling creeds!

                    THOMAS CURTIS CLARK

THUS SPEAKETH CHRIST OUR LORD

*(Engraved on an old slab in the Cathedral
of Lübeck, Germany)*

Ye call Me Master and obey Me not,
Ye call Me Light and see Me not,
Ye call Me Way and walk not,
Ye call Me Life and desire Me not,
Ye call Me wise and follow Me not,
Ye call Me fair and love Me not,
Ye call Me rich and ask Me not,
Ye call Me eternal and seek Me not,
Ye call Me gracious and trust Me not,
Ye call Me noble and serve Me not,
Ye call Me mighty and honor Me not,
Ye call Me just and fear Me not.
If I condemn you, blame Me not.

ANONYMOUS

IF HE SHOULD COME

If Jesus should tramp the streets tonight,
  Storm-beaten and hungry for bread,
Seeking a room and a candle light
  And a clean though humble bed,
Who would welcome the Workman in,
  Though he came with panting breath,
His hands all bruised and his garments thin—
  This Workman from Nazareth?

Would rich folk hurry to bind his bruise
    And shelter his stricken form?
Would they take God in with his muddy shoes
    Out of the pitiless storm?
Are they not too busy wreathing their flowers
    Or heaping their golden store—
Too busy chasing the bubble hours
    For the poor man's God at the door?

And if he should come where churchmen bow,
    Forgetting the greater sin,
Would he pause with a light on his wounded brow,
    Would he turn and enter in?
And what would he think of their creeds so dim,
    Of their weak, uplifted hands,
Of their selfish prayers going up to him
    Out of a thousand lands?

EDWIN MARKHAM

FROM "IF JESUS CAME BACK TODAY"

If Jesus came back today
What would the people say?
Would they cheer him and strew the way
With garlands of myrtle and bay
As they did on that distant day
When he came to Jerusalem?
What would America say
If Jesus came back today?

We fashion great churches and creeds
But the heart of the people still bleeds
And the poor still rot in their needs.
We display with pride his cross
In the midst of our pagan life
While we hug to our hearts the dross
Of our selfishness and strife.
What sacrifice have we made
To live the love he prayed?
What willing blood have we shed
To do the deeds he said?
To be popular and well fed
We forsake the way he led
And follow a ghost instead!

VINCENT GODFREY BURNS

EARTH BOWS TO THE NEW BOMB

What power is this released in man's dark night
  Upon the world where blood was sacrificed?
Has earth forgotten him who healed men's sight,
  The power of Selfless Love in One called Christ?

ALINE BADGER CARTER

The Triumphant Christ

FROM "IN MEMORIAM"

Strong Son of God, immortal Love,
    Whom we, that have not seen thy face,
    By faith, and faith alone, embrace,
Believing where we cannot prove;

Thine are these orbs of light and shade;
    Thou madest Life in man and brute;
    Thou madest Death; and lo, thy foot
Is on the skull which thou hast made.

Thou wilt not leave us in the dust:
    Thou madest man, he knows not why,
    He thinks he was not made to die;
And Thou hast made him: thou art just.

Thou seemest human and divine,
    The highest, holiest manhood, thou.
    Our wills are ours, we know not how;
Our wills are ours, to make them thine.

ALFRED TENNYSON

THE ETERNAL WORD

In the beginning was the Word;
    Athwart the Chaos, night;
It gleamed with quick creative power
    And there was life and light.

Thy Word, O God, is living yet
  Amid earth's restless strife,
New harmony creating still
  And ever higher life.

O Word that broke the stillness first,
  Sound on, and never cease
Till all earth's darkness be made light,
  And all her discord peace.

Till selfish passion, strife and wrong,
  Thy summons shall have heard,
And Thy creation be complete,
  O Thou Eternal Word.
    HENRY WADSWORTH LONGFELLOW

FROM "COPLAS DE MANRIQUE"

To One alone my thoughts arise,
The Eternal Truth,—the Good and Wise—
To Him I cry,
Who shared on earth our common lot,
But the world comprehended not
His deity.
    HENRY WADSWORTH LONGFELLOW

NO PRISONER OF TIME

Christ was no prisoner of time,
  His truth transcends each age;
His words beyond compare, sublime;
  His life, life's deathless page.
      WILLIAM H. HUDNUT, JR.

CREDO

Not what, but *Whom,* I do believe,
   That, in my darkest hour of need,
   Hath comfort that no mortal creed
   To mortal man may give;—
Not what, but *Whom!*
   For Christ is more than all the creeds,
   And his full life of gentle deeds
   Shall all the creeds outlive.

Not what I do believe, but *Whom!*
   Who walks beside me in the gloom?
   Who shares the burden wearisome?
   Who all the dim way doth illume,
   And bids me look beyond the tomb
   The larger life to live?—
Not what I do believe,
   But *Whom!*
   Not what
   But *Whom!*

                     JOHN OXENHAM

FROM "THE RING AND THE BOOK"

           No one ever plucked
A rag even, from the body of the Lord,
To wear and mock with, but despite himself
He looked the greater and was the better.

                     ROBERT BROWNING

A CREED

Here is the Truth in a little creed,
    Enough for all the roads we go:
In Love is all the law we need,
    In Christ is all the God we know.
EDWIN MARKHAM

CHRIST'S REIGN OF PEACE

And he shall charm and soothe, and breathe and
    bless,
The roaring of war shall cease upon the air,
Falling of tears and all the voices of sorrow,
And he shall take the terror from the grave.

And he shall still that old sob of the sea,
And heal the unhappy fancies of the wind,
And turn the moon from all that hopeless quest;
Trees without care shall blossom, and all the fields
Shall without labor unto harvest come.
STEPHEN PHILLIPS

BRINGERS OF THE HEMLOCK

They thought to kill old Socrates: instead,
    They launched his name on an immortal tide.
Ten million, blotted out, lie stony dead,
    But one Man lived the more because he died.
STANTON A. COBLENTZ

THE DISCIPLE

I could not leave Thee, Christ! For when I tried
To leave Thee for alluring ways aside
From Thine own way, Thy power withheld me, kept
My feet from wandering too far, inept
And aimless, down a dwindling path that led
Through mazed confusion to the house of dread.

I could not leave Thee, Christ! For when I yearned
With passionate intensity and burned
With fiery torment to assuage my thirst
For freedom by a turbid stream that burst
In gushing torrents from a naked hill—
Thou ledst me back to waters deep and still.

I could not leave Thee, Christ! For when I sought
To fling aside Thy counsel, when I thought
That in my crazy freedom I should find
Some way of life for body, soul and mind
Better than Thou didst teach, I heard Thee say,
"Come back to Me, for thou hast lost thy way."

I would not leave Thee, Christ! For I am lame
From wandering, and the consuming flame
Of passion has gone out and left my soul
A smoldering ember, and the criss-crossed scroll
Of life ends as it started with the line,
"I cannot leave Thee, Christ! For I am Thine."

DWIGHT BRADLEY

"HE THAT DOETH THE WILL"

From all vain pomps and shows,
From the pride that overflows,
And the false conceits of men;
From all the narrow rules
And subtleties of Schools,
And the craft of tongue and pen;
Bewildered in its search,
Bewildered with the cry:
Lo, here! Lo, there, the Church!
Poor, sad humanity
Through all the dust and heat
Turns back with bleeding feet,
By the weary road it came,
Unto the simple thought
By the great Master taught,
And that remaineth still:
Not he that repeateth the name,
But he that doeth the will!

HENRY WADSWORTH LONGFELLOW

LOYALTY HYMN

While nations rage, while empires rock and fall,
   While hatred burns, and greed and war increase,
With heart and voice we dedicate our all
   Once more to Thee, O mighty Prince of Peace.
Fast grow abysmal rifts in every land,
   O'er creed and class, o'er wealth and soil and
     blood.
Through all the earth, made one in Thee, we stand—
   Thy Church in its transcendent brotherhood.

Into the soon forgotten past they die,
    False gods that rise and flourish for a day.
Not so Thy Cross, firm rooted in the sky;
    Thy words, O Christ, shall never pass away.

While nations rage, while empires rock and fall,
    While hatred burns, and greed and war increase,
With heart and voice we dedicate our all
    Once more to Thee, O mighty Prince of Peace.

EDITH LOVEJOY PIERCE

Index of Authors

114

116

Index of Titles